TG186630

101 Simple Truths
for Creating a Passionate Life

. . . a handbook for the passionate soul

Teri Shaughnessy

iUniverse, Inc.
New York   Bloomington

iUniverse books may be ordered through booksellers or by contacting:

iUniverse
1663 Liberty Drive
Bloomington, IN 47403
www.iuniverse.com
1-800-Authors (1-800-288-4677)

ISBN: 978-1-4401-6504-7 (pbk)
ISBN: 978-1-4401-6505-4 (ebk)

Printed in the United States of America

iUniverse rev. date: 8/6/2009

This book is dedicated to Joel Henderson. His support, encouragement, and patience have allowed me to follow my heart and live my passions each and every day. To you Joel, I am forever grateful.

A big thanks to my Master Mind partner, Patty Richardson, for contributing the fun and whimsical illustrations seen throughout this book.

Preface

Living a passionate life, a life with purpose and meaning, doesn't have to be daunting. There are simple actions you can take every day, which over time, will bring joy and fulfillment to your life.

I wrote this book to offer you simple ways of approaching your day. Some require more time than others. Some you may already be doing. I feel these simple Truths will speak to your heart and be reminders about some of the most basic gestures we can make in our daily lives.

These Truths are not in any particular order. There's not one that is more important than the other, except how you view them. Some may seem silly to you and others may speak to your soul.

My hope is that these Truths will inspire you, comfort you, and maybe even bring a smile to your face. It has been my experience in creating my passionate life, that simple gestures of self-love and reaching out to those less fortunate will lead you to living a purpose-filled life.

I hope you will enjoy!

To passionate living!

Teri Shaughnessy, Life Success Coach

"Passion has the power to transform your life. When you discover your deepest passions, you connect with the essence of who you are. Living life aligned with your passions, your personal destiny unfolds naturally and effortlessly."

"The Passion Test" by Janet Bray Attwood & Chris Attwood

Truth #1: Take the Passion Test

Truth #2: Create time for yourself
and someone you love each day.

"When we recall the past, we usually find that it is the simplest things – not the great occasions – that in retrospect give off the greatest glow of happiness.

Bob Hope, America's No. 1 Soldier in Greasepaint, one of the greatest entertainers to the U.S. Troupes all over the world.

Truth #3: Write in a journal daily and read what you wrote at least quarterly.

"I never want to be

What I want to be,

Because there's always something out there

yet for me.

There's always one hill higher
--- with a better view,

Something waiting to be learned I never
knew. So until my days are over Never fully
fill my cup. Let me keep growing --- up."

Art Linkletter, Host & Author of
"Kids Say the Darndest Things."

Truth #4: Be dedicated
to life-long learning.

"I'm not handsome in the classical sense. The eyes droop, the mouth is crooked, the teeth aren't straight, the voice sounds like a mafioso pallbearer."

Sylvester Stalone – "*Rocky*" et al

Truth #5: Floss regularly.

"A Code of Honor consists of rules that we all take seriously, that we commit to and that we hold ourselves accountable to. In other words, we walk our talk. It becomes our badge of honor."

Blair Singer, Sales Communication Specialist & Author of "Sales Dogs."

Truth #6: Create your OWN
Code of Honor to live by.

"Seize the moment. Remember all those women on the Titanic who waved off the dessert cart."

Erma Bombeck, American Humorist

Truth #7: Eat a luscious dessert once a week --- with no regret.

"No one can make you feel inferior without your permission."

Eleanor Roosevelt – American First Lady & Humanitarian

Truth #8: Never concern yourself with the opinion of others as it says more about them than it does about you.

"Our duty as human beings is to proceed
as if our limits to our abilities do not exist."

Anonymous

Truth #9: Take Risks.

"A happy heart makes the face cheerful . . .
the cheerful heart has a continual feast."

Proverbs 15:13, 15.

Truth #10: Smile at a stranger every day.

"Fashions fade, style is eternal."

Yves Saint Laurent,
French Fashion Designer

Truth #11: Dress for Success.

"Seek first to understand. Before
the problems come up, before you try
to evaluate & prescribe, before you
try to present your own ideas---seek
to understand. It's a powerful habit
of effective interdependence."

Stephen R. Covey, Author, "The 7
Habits of Highly Effective People."

Truth #12: When in a conflict, listen to the other person. Strive to understand the other person first. Then voice your concerns.

"Until we can see what we thought happened, didn't, there is no forgiveness. We try to have lighter hearts & overlook it, but that's not forgiveness. To see what you thought happened, didn't, that's forgiveness & it is complete."

Byron Katie, Author of *"Loving What Is"* & Teacher, www.thework.com

Truth #13: Forgive.

"It's really hard to walk in a single woman's shoes – that's why you sometimes need really special shoes."

Carrie Bradshaw from "Sex and the City."

Truth #14: Wear fun shoes.

"All, everything that I understand, I understand only because I love."

Leo Tolstoy, Author of "*War and Peace.*"

Truth #15: Make Love Often.

"Ask, and it shall be given to you;

Seek, and ye shall find;

Knock and it shall be opened unto you.

For every one that asketh, receiveth;

And he that seeketh, findeth;

And to him that knocketh
it shall be opened."

Matthew 7: 7-8

Truth #16: Ask for What You Want & Believe that You Deserve it.

"Greatness at all levels is bred out of accountability. As a parent, spouse, business owner, leader, teammate, or friend, honestly looking at your actions and holding yourself accountable to them determines the quality and standards of your life."

Blair Singer, Sales Communication Specialist, Author of "The ABC's of Building a Business Team That Wins."

Truth #17: Honor Your Agreements.

"One wonders what would happen in a society in which there were no rules to break. Doubtless everyone would quickly die of boredom."

Susan Howatch – British writer

Truth #18: Break a Silly Rule.

"There's a four-letter word you must use when you get rejected -- NEXT!"

Jack Canfield, America's
#1 Success Coach

Truth #19: Never Berate Yourself.

"We need your service right now, at
this moment in history. I'm not going to
tell you what your role should be; that's
for you to discover. But I'm asking you
to stand up and play your part."

Barak Obama, after signing
the Edward M. Kennedy Serve
America Act, April 22, 2009

Truth #20: Volunteer for some event that forces you out of your comfort zone.

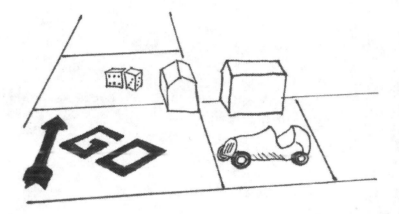

Truth #21: Play games such as Monopoly, Twister, Life, Bocce Ball with your family.

(Your relationship with your spouse or lover) . . . "And this is the most intimate, the most potentially rich, joyful, satisfying and productive relationship possible between two people on this earth."

Stephen R. Covey, Author, "The Seven Habits of Highly Effective People."

Truth #22: Love your Partner
With All Your Heart.

"If you want to know if your brain
is flabby, feel your legs."

Bruce Barton – Journalist
and Advertising Guru

Truth #23: Walk the stairs instead of taking the elevator.

"For variety of mere nothings gives more pleasure than uniformity of something."

Jean Paul Ritcher

Truth #24: Drive home a different way at least once a week.

Truth #25: At some point in your life, adopt a dog or cat.

"Whoever wants to know the heart and mind of America had better learn baseball, the rules and realities of the game and do it by watching first some high-school or small-town teams."

Jacques Barzun, French Educator, born 1907

Truth #26: Go to High School
or College sports events even
if your kids aren't playing.

Truth #27: Plant a tree and watch it grow.

"Walking inspires and promotes conversation that is grounded in the body, and so it gives the soul a place where it can thrive. I think I could write an interesting memoir of significant walks I have taken with others, in which intimacy was not only experienced but set fondly into the landscape of memory."

Thomas Moore, "*Soul Mates.*"

Truth #28: Regularly take a walk with
a friend, your spouse, or partner.

"Once you begin to acknowledge random acts of kindness - both the ones you have received and the ones you have given - you can no longer believe that what you do does not matter."

- Dawna Markova, Author of "The Open Mind"

Truth #29: Buy a coffee, tea or soda for someone who won't expect it.

"If I'd known I was gonna live this long.
I'd have taken better care of myself."
[Eubie Blake At Age 100]

Eubie Blake – Ragtime & Jazz composer

Truth #30: Get a massage regularly.

" . . . that is the best . . .to laugh with someone because you both think the same things are funny."

Anonymous (a very special friend)

Truth #31: Join a club that surrounds you with the things you love doing and with the people you most enjoy.

"Do men who have got all their marbles go swimming in lakes with their clothes on?"

P.G. Wodehouse – Comic writer, playwright & lyricist

Truth #32: Skinny dip.

Truth #33: Save, but never for a rainy day.

"You get what you *feel* about
what you think about."

Esther and Jerry Hicks, Author "The
Amazing Power of Deliberate Intent."

Truth #34: Act as if what you want you already have.

"Simply put, the Law of Attraction says that you will attract into your life whatever you focus on. Whatever you give your energy and attention to will come back to you."

Jack Canfield, America's No. 1 Success Coach

Truth #35: Learn how to apply the Law of Attraction.

"A good laugh and a long sleep are the best cures in the doctor's book."

Irish Proverb

Truth #36: Sleep in at least once a week.

"We make a living by what we get, but
we make a life by what we give."

Winston Churchill, Prime Minister

Truth #37: Share.

"Be the change you want
to see in the world."

Mahatma Gandhi

Truth #38: When in line or in heavy traffic, allow someone to move ahead of you.

Truth #39: Dance as if no one is watching.

"The jump is so frightening between where I am and where I want to be . . . because of all I may become. I will close my eyes and leap!"

Maryann Hershey, 1992,
Cannon Beach Oregon

Truth #40: No Guts, No Glory.

Truth #41: Close Your Eyes
and Listen to Mozart.

"She did observe with some dismay, that, far from conquering all, love lazily sidestepped practical problems."

Jean Stafford, an American writer

Truth #42: Fall in Love again
and again and again.

" . . . you may be disappointed if you fail,
but you are doomed if you don't try."

Anonymous

Truth #43: Never, ever, under any circumstances, never give up.

"Don't sweat the small stuff .
. . and it's all small stuff."

Richard Carlson, Ph.D.

Truth #44: Don't take anything too seriously.

Truth #45: Have a favorite pair
of jeans throughout your life.

"Every child is an artist. The problem is how to remain an artist after growing up."

Roger von Oech from "A Whack on the Side of the Head"

Truth #46: Create something – a poem,
a dessert, a sculpture, a garden, a dream,
a new recipe, a design, a love letter.

Truth #47: Buy yourself a bouquet of flowers at least once a month.

"If the person you are talking to doesn't appear to be listening be patient. It may simply be that he has a small piece of fluff in his ear."

Winnie the Pooh

Truth #48: Kiss Your Children and Look Them in the Eye to Tell Them You Love Them Every Day.

"The wounds of sour words, disgusting glances, and maimed emotions are not to be allowed to swirl the night in slumber."

Teri Shaughnessy, Author, Public Speaker & Founder of, *No Guts, No Glory* – www.nogutsnoglory.org

Truth #49: Never Go to Bed
Angry at Someone.

Truth #50: Stretch your body.

"It is said that a thankful heart is not
only the greatest virtue, but also
the parent of all other virtues."

Anonymous

Truth #51: Say please & thank you.

"If one advances confidently in the direction of his dreams, and endeavors to live the life he has imagined, he will meet with a success unexpected in common hours."

Henry David Thoreau

Truth #52: Walk with grace & determination.

Truth #53: Take a nap on your day off.

"A real friend is one who walks in when
the rest of the world walks out."

Walter Winchell, Journalist & Narrator
of the T.V. hit, "The Untouchables

Truth #54: Spend an afternoon with a friend at least once a month.

"There are only two ways to live your life. One is as though nothing is a miracle. The other is as though everything is a miracle."

Albert Einstein

Truth #55: Appreciate the little
gifts that come your way.

Truth #56: Keep your childhood teddy bear close by.

"Take the gentle path."

George Herbert – Early 17th century poet

Truth #57: When someone compliments you, simply say thank you.

"Call it a clan, call it a network, call it a tribe, call it a family. Whatever you call it, whoever you are, you need one."

Jane Howard, U.S. Journalist & Author

Truth #58: Do the dishes with
your family & share the day.

"Life is short, take a bath."

Teri Shaughnessy, Life Coach & Author of "101 Truths for Living a Passionate Life."

Truth #59: Take a bubble bath
with a lighted candle.

"Maintaining a steady flow of fresh air into your bedroom will decrease the likelihood of you developing insomnia, because you won't be re-breathing the same stale air over and over again."

www.slumbo.com

Truth #60: Let some fresh
air in while sleeping.

"The will of God will never take you where the Grace of God will not protect you."

Author unknown.

Truth #61: Day dream.

"Wine is bottled poetry."

Robert Louis Stevenson-Scottish poet & Author of "Treasure Island."

Truth #62: Choose a wine for
its label, not its price.

"I left my heart in San Francisco

High on a hill, it calls to me.

To be where little cable cars

Climb halfway to the stars!

The morning fog may chill the air

I don't care!

My love waits there in San Francisco

Above the blue and windy sea

When I come home to you, San Francisco,

Your golden sun will shine for me!"

Tony Bennett---Bennett performed "I Left My Heart in San Francisco" for the first time in 1962 at the Fairmont Hotel on Nob Hill in San Francisco, and it quickly became his signature song.

Truth #63: Visit San Francisco

"Fear always springs from ignorance."

Ralph Waldo Emerson

Truth #64: Ask a lot of questions.

"Traditions create memories. Memories create stories. Stories create connections to those we cherish in our hearts."

Theresa L. Shaughnessy – an Irish lass

Truth #65: Create a family tradition and keep to it. Your children will never forget it.

"Studies have suggested that too little sleep (less than 7 hours each night) reduces your life expectancy."

www.medicalnewstoday.com

Truth #66: Sleep eight hours a night.

"I never met a weed I didn't love."

Gale deLong, my dear friend &
Sonoma County gardener & artist

Truth #67: Weed your garden.

"Unless commitment is made, there are only promises and hopes; but no plans."

Peter Drucker, American Educator and writer

Truth #68: Make a commitment that is incredibly important to you.

"Often people attempt to live their lives backwards: they try to have more things, or more money, in order to do more of what they want so that they will be happier. The way it actually works is the reverse. You must first be who you really are, then, do what you need to do, in order to have what you want."

Margaret Young, Popular American singer in the 1920s

Truth #69: Create your authentic
self and allow yourself to be her/
him every moment of your day.

"Every one has the capability of playing and winning a big game. Not everyone will. Little voices will determine that outcome."

Blair Singer, Author –
"'Little Voice' Mastery."

Truth #70: Learn to manage your "little voice" – the one that gets in the way of accomplishing even the smallest things.

"Variety is the soul of pleasure."

Aphra Behn – British Professional Writer

Truth #71: Do something a little different from the way you've always done it. Use whole wheat pasta instead of white, grapefruit juice instead of orange, tea instead of coffee. Be creative!

"Every failure brings with it the Seed
of an Equivalent Success."

Napoleon Hill, Author –
"Think and Grow Rich"

Truth #72: Be willing to fail.

"When we give something for the pure pleasure of giving, our feelings of generosity inspire others to be generous."

Arnold M. Patent, Author ~
"You Can Have It All"

Truth #73: Always be more generous than the last time.

"Nothing happens ahead of its time. It happens on time. Not your time, on time."

Byron Katie, Author – "Who Would You be Without Your Story."

Truth #74: Live in the moment. All
we truly have is this moment.

Truth #75: Create memories
for your child or grandchild.

"Someone once said, ' "No pain, no gain." ' And so it became their reality. Bummer, huh?"

Mike Dooley, Featured in "The Secret" and Author of "Notes from the Universe"

Truth #76: Question your
stressful thoughts.

"When someone pays you a compliment and your little voice starts chirping away with excuses, you are robbing yourself of a win and putting the brakes on acknowledging and leveraging your strengths."

Blair Singer, Author, " 'Little Voice' Mastery"

Truth #77: Be ready & willing to receive compliments, gifts, smiles, love, and watch your life flourish.

"Change the way you look at things
and the things you look at change."

Wayne Dyer, Author and
Transformational leader

Truth #78: Embrace change.

"With everything that has happened
to you, you can either feel sorry for
yourself, or treat what has happened as a
gift. Everything is either an opportunity
to grow or an obstacle to keep you
from growing. You get to choose."

Wayne Dyer, Author, Transformational
Leader – *"Staying on the Path"*

Truth #79: Understand that
scarcity is self-imposed.

"Feel the Fear . . . . And Do It Anyway."
Susan Jeffers, Ph.D.

Truth #80: Face your fears head-on.

Truth #81: Take time each day to give yourself something you need – a long bath, a hug from your child, a 10 minute power nap, 30 minutes to exercise or to read a good novel.

"The measure of your life will not be in what you accumulate, but what you give away."

Wayne Dyer, Author, Transformational Leader, "Staying on the Path"

Truth #82: Tithe 10 of your income.

"Friendship," said Pooh, "is a very comforting sort of thing."

Winnie the Pooh sharing a walk with Tiger

Truth #83: Maintain your relationship
with your best friend forever.

"What a gift of grace to be able to take the chaos from within and from it create some semblance of order."

--Katherine Patterson, Author of Juvenile Fiction

Truth #84: Get rid of clutter.
Keep a simple life.

"Your relationship is a precious jewel. Not everyone has been given such a gift. Treasure it, hold it in your hand and up to the light, and let its extraordinary beauty open your heart and transform your life."

Daphne Rose Kingma – Psychotherapist & Bestselling Author

Truth #85: Love unconditionally.

"The lack of emotional security of our American young people is due, I believe, to their isolation from the larger family unit. No two people - no mere father and mother - as I have often said, are enough to provide emotional security for a child. He needs to feel himself one in a world of kinfolk, persons of variety in age and temperament, and yet allied to himself by an indissoluble bond which he cannot break if he could, for nature has welded him into it before he was born."

--- Pearl S. Buck, Author & Philanthropist

Truth #86: Go to the zoo with
your children and/or grandchildren.
Watch your relationship blossom.

"Color represents freedom and joy. It soothes the soul and excites the heart."

Author unknown

Truth #87: Paint a wall in your home a color that best represents your spirit & sense of adventure.

"Take Time for Your Life."

Cheryl Richardson

Truth #88: Decorate a real
spruce tree at Christmas time.

"Just slow down."

Ed Begley Jr. – Actor & Activist

Truth #89: Take 10 minutes a
day for quiet reflection.

"No act of kindness, no matter
how small, is ever wasted."

Aesop

Truth #90: Bake chocolate chip cookies,
eat one and give the rest away.

"Our duty as human beings is to proceed as if limits to our abilities do not exist."

Anonymous – taken from *The Hear of a Lion.* By Bill O'Hearn

Truth #91: Get rid of the struggle.

"If I had a world of my own, everything would be nonsense. Nothing would be what it is, because everything would be what it isn't. And contrary wise, what is, it wouldn't be. And what it wouldn't be, it would. You see?"

Alice in *"Alice in Wonderland."*

Truth #92: Instead of killing that moth, capture it and send it on its way.

"If you want happiness for
an hour -- take a nap.

If you want happiness for a day -- go fishing.

If you want happiness for a
month -- get married.

If you want happiness for a
lifetime -- help others."

Christine Comaford-Lynch –
"Rules for Renegades"

Truth #93: Become the person people want and need.

"Your attitude determines your altitude."

Stephen R. Covey

Truth #94: Check in on your
attitude. It will determine your day.

"Laughter is the closest distance between two people."

Victor Borge, American Comedian & Pianist

Truth #95: Laugh often.

"We sat at this point & let

our eyes wander across the canyon.

All worries seeped away into the

stony stillness & there was silence."

Gena McCafferty, an Ireland visitor
commenting on the Grand Canyon

Truth #96: Visit the Grand Canyon with someone you love.

"The universe operates through dynamic exchange--giving and receiving are different aspects of the flow of energy in the universe. And in our willingness to give that which we seek, we keep the abundance of the universe circulating in our lives."

Deepak Chopra, "The Seven Spiritual Laws of Success"

Truth #97: Spread your abundance
by paying a toll for the car behind you,
contributing to Boys & Girls clubs, serving
food at the homeless shelters on a holiday.

"Love can touch us one time
and last for a life time."

Lyrics from theme song from *The Titanic*

Truth #98: Have unconditional love for yourself.

"Gratitude can lead you, as it did me, away from the darkness of complicated need into the light of simple abundance."

Sarah Ban Breathnack, Author, "The Simple Abundance Journal of Gratitude."

Truth #99: Express your appreciation
& gratitude for your blessings,
challenges, struggles, & triumphs.

"Kind words can be short and easy to speak but their echoes are truly endless."

Mother Teresa

Truth #100: Be kind when you don't feel like it, as everyone you encounter is battling a challenge in their life today.

"Before you score, you must
first have a goal."

Greek Proverb

Truth #101: Create measurable goals for yourself and make a commitment to them.